Beginner English

30 Short Stories Written For Beg

by Camille Hanson

LEARN ENGLISH WITH *Camille*

LearnEnglishwithCamille.com

Editor: Christine Irvine - instagram.com/FactsAboutEnglish
Book design & layout: Calvin Hanson - CalvinHansonCreative.com

---

ISBN 9798882958342 (paperback)
Independently Published
First printing 2024
Copyright © 2024

Table of Contents

How to use this book

This is a book of beginner level short stories. Most of them are 150-200 words and written with real life English words and phrases. Some of these stories are 100% true, and some of them are fiction. There is a note next to each real story. Learning English through stories is an amazing way to advance in your language learning journey. You will learn vocabulary and grammar, such as sentence structure and prepositions, all while having fun. Read each story. Highlight any new words. Don't worry about trying to understand every single word. Try to understand the main ideas. At the end of each story, there is a true and false quiz, a multiple choice quiz, and a fill in the blank quiz. Answers to the activities can be found at the end of each story.

There is a link for printable flashcards with small pictures so that you can practice learning new vocabulary words from the stories. Be sure to listen to the free audio that accompanies each story. Read the stories as many times as you would like. Use the note section in the back of the book to practice writing your own short stories in English.

As always, happy learning.

Get your audio download & flashcards!

GO TO <u>PAGE 83</u>

NOTE: This is so Amazon Preview viewers can't download free audio or flashcards. I appreciate your support and for learning with me! ~ Camille

Story 1 **My House** TRUE STORY

I (Camille) live in Portugal. Portugal is in Europe, next to Spain. I live in a small city on the sea. There are many cars that drive on our street. I live in a big house. It is yellow and white. My house has two floors. It has four bedrooms, four bathrooms, a kitchen, and a living room. There are many windows.

I like my house. My house has a yard with a lot of trees. There is an orange tree. There is also an avocado tree. I like to eat the fruit from the trees. The fruit is very good. I like to sit outside and watch my children play. We have a small pool. In the summer, my kids swim in the pool. They have fun. We have a garage, and we park our car in the garage. Our car is blue. We are happy here. We like our house, our yard, and our car.

True/False

Is the statement below true or false? Write T for true or F for false.

1. Camille lives in Portugal. _____
2. Portugal is in South America. _____
3. The house in the story has one floor. _____
4. There is a mango tree in the yard. _____

5. The family parks their car on the street. _____

Multiple Choice

Circle the correct answer

1. Where does Camille live?

a) Spain

b) Portugal

c) France

d) Italy

2. How many floors does the house have?

a) One

b) Two

c) Three

d) Four

3. What color is the family's car?

a) Yellow

b) Blue

c) Red

d) Green

4. What type of fruit tree is in the yard?

a) Mango

b) Pear

c) Avocado

d) Apple

5. Where do the children swim in the summer?

a) Lake

b) Ocean

c) Pool

d) River

Fill in the blank

Fill in the blank with the sentences below.

1. Portugal is in _____. Asia / Europe / South America

2. There are many cars that drive _____ the street. on / at / over

3. Camille lives in a big white _____. car / house / apartment

4. The yard has _____ tree. cherry and an orange / an avocado and a pear / an orange and an avocado

5. The kids _____ in the pool. run / sleep / swim

Answers

True/False 1. T 2. F 3. F 4. F 5. F

Multiple Choice 1.b) Portugal 2. b) Two 3. b) Blue 4. c) Avocado 5. c) Pool

Fill in the blank 1. Europe 2. on 3. house 4. an orange/an avocado 5. swim

Story 2 **Camille's Family** TRUE STORY

My name is Camille. I am married. My husband's name is Calvin. I am his wife. We have three children. Their names are Maddox, Ivory, and Kairo. Maddox is ten years old, Ivory is seven years old, and Kairo is five years old. Maddox is the oldest child. Ivory is the middle child. Kairo is the youngest child. We call the youngest child "the baby." Maddox and Kairo are boys. They are brothers. Ivory is a girl. She is Maddox and Kairo's sister. Maddox and Kairo are Ivory's brothers. Maddox, Ivory, and Kairo are siblings.

My parents are named Tom and Helen. Helen is my mother. Tom is my father. I am their daughter. Helen is my kids' grandmother (grandma). Tom is my kids' grandfather (grandpa). They are my children's grandparents. They love my children. My children love their grandparents.

True/False

Is the statement below true or false? Write T for true or F for false.

1. Camille is married to Calvin. _____
2. Maddox is the youngest child. _____
3. Ivory is Maddox and Kairo's sister. _____
4. Tom and Helen are Camille's children. _____

5. Ivory is the middle child. _____

Multiple Choice

Circle the correct answer

1. Who is Camille married to?

a) Maddox

b) Calvin

c) Ivory

d) Kairo

2. How many children do Camille and Calvin have?

a) Two

b) Three

c) Four

d) Five

3. Who is the oldest child?

a) Maddox

b) Ivory

c) Kairo

d) Not specified

4. What is Maddox and Kairo's relationship?

a) Cousins

b) Neighbors

c) Friends

d) Brothers

5. Who are Tom and Helen to Camille's children?

a) Parents

b) Grandparents

c) Siblings

d) Friends

Fill in the blank

Fill in the blank with the sentences below.

1. Camille's _____ name is Calvin. friend's / husband's / sister's

2. Ivory is seven _____ old. years / days / months

3. The youngest child is called _____. kid / toddler / the baby

4. Another name for grandmother is _____. grandma / mom / mother

5. My children _____ their grandparents. hate / love / like

Answers

True/False 1. T 2. F 3. T 4. F 5. T

Multiple Choice 1.b) Calvin 2. b) Three 3. a) Maddox 4. d) Brothers 5. b) Grandparents

Fill in the blank 1. husband's 2. years 3. the baby 4. grandma 5. love

Story 3 **My Jobs** TRUE STORY

I have many jobs. My first job is being a mom. I am a stay-at-home-mom to three children, so I take care of my kids every day. I play with them, I cook food for them, and I wash their clothes. I also homeschool my children. I teach them math, science, and reading at home. It's a big job. My second job is a content creator. I write English books, create English videos, and create English courses. I like to help people learn English. My third job is a host. I rent my house in America with the company Airbnb. Airbnb is a place where you can rent your house. People send me messages when they want to rent my house. There is a woman that cleans my rental house. I have a lot of jobs, but I am not Superwoman. I have help. My husband's name is Calvin. He helps me with all three of my jobs. I am so happy that he helps me. Together we are a good team. We are both good at our jobs.

True/False

Is the statement below true or false? Write T for true or F for false.

1. Camille's first job is being a stay-at-home mom. _____
2. Camille homeschools her children. _____

3. Camille's second job is as a chef. _____

4. Calvin does not help Camille with her jobs. _____

5. Camille thinks she is Superwoman. _____

Multiple Choice

Circle the correct answer

1. What is Camille's second job?

a) Content creator

b) Chef

c) Stay-at-home mom

d) Teacher

2. What does Camille do as a content creator?

a) Creates English courses

b) Writes English books

c) Creates Videos

d) All of the above

3. How does Camille earn money from her house in America?

a) Selling it

b) Renting it out through Airbnb

c) Using it as a vacation home

d) Turning it into a museum

4. Who helps Camille with her jobs?

a) Her children

b) Her parents

c) Her husband Calvin

d) Her neighbors

5. What does Camille do as an Airbnb host?

a) Responds to messages through Airbnb

b) Cleans the rental houses

c) Creates English courses

d) Teaches math and science

Fill in the blank

Fill in the blank with the sentences below.

1. Camille _____ food for her children. cooks / eats / throws away

2. She _____ her children's clothes. loses / washes / ruins

3. Camille _____ her house in America. rents / sells / destroys

4. There is a _____ that cleans the rental house. man / cousin / woman

5. Camille and Calvin are a good _____. friend / relationship / team

Answers

True/False 1. T 2. T 3. F 4. F 5. F

Multiple Choice 1. a) Content creator 2. d) All of the above 3. b) Renting it out through Airbnb 4. c) Her husband Calvin 5. a) Responds to messages through Airbnb

Fill in the blank 1. cooks 2. washes 3. rents 4. woman 5. team

Story 4 **Seasons**

There are four seasons in the United States. Each season has a name. There is winter, spring, summer, and fall. I enjoy every season. Winter starts in December. It is cold in the winter, and sometimes it snows. Snow is white. It also rains in many places in the winter. Take an umbrella with you when you go places. I like winter because we celebrate Christmas in December, but I do not like cold weather. Spring starts in March. In spring the weather starts to warm up. People plant flowers and vegetables. Spring is a beautiful time of the year. Summer starts in June. Summer is hot. It's a good time to go swimming. Summer vacation is also nice. Fall starts in September. The weather starts to get colder in the fall. The leaves change colors. They change from green to red, orange, and yellow. They are so pretty. Then the leaves start to fall off the trees. Fall is my favorite season. It's not too cold, and I can wear sweaters. Those are the four seasons.

True/False

Is the statement below true or false? Write T for true or F for false.

1. There are five seasons in the United States. _____

2. Winter starts in December. _____

3. Snow is usually black. _____

4. Fall is Camille's favorite season. _____

5. Leaves fall off the trees in the spring. _____

Multiple Choice

Circle the correct answer

1. When does summer start?

   a) March

   b) June

   c) December

   d) September

2. What color are the leaves in fall?

   a) Green

   b) Red, orange, and yellow

   c) Blue

   d) Purple

3. What happens to the leaves in fall?

   a) They grow bigger.

   b) They change colors and fall off.

   c) They turn black.

   d) They turn white.

4. When is summer vacation?

   a) April

   b) March

   c) August

   d) September

5. Which season is good for swimming?

   a) Winter

   b) Spring

   c) Fall

   d) Summer

Fill in the blank

Fill in the blank with the sentences below.

1. There are _____ seasons in the United States.

four/three/two

2. It is _____ in the winter. warm / hot / cold

3. _____ starts in March. Fall / Winter / Spring

4. Summer starts in _____. June / September / December

5. The leaves _____ colors. fall / become / change

_____

Answers

True/False 1. F 2. T 3. F 4. T 5. F

Multiple Choice 1. b) June 2. b) Red, orange, and yellow 3. b) They change colors and fall off 4. c) August 5. d) Summer

Fill in the blank 1. four 2. cold 3. Spring 4. June 5. change

Story 5 **Sam is Hungry**

Sam wakes up. Sam is very hungry. It is time for breakfast. He wants to eat some food. He walks to his kitchen, and he opens his fridge. He sees eggs, but he doesn't want eggs. He is tired of eggs. Sam sees some yogurt, but he doesn't want yogurt. Sam closes his fridge. He sees bananas on his counter. He likes bananas. Sam takes a banana, and he peels it. He eats the banana. Sam throws the banana peel in the garbage. Sam is still hungry. Sam sees another banana. He peels the banana. He eats the banana. Now Sam is thirsty. He opens the fridge. He sees milk and orange juice, but he doesn't want milk or orange juice. He wants water. He turns on the sink and fills a glass with water. He drinks it all. It tastes so good. Sam is happy. He puts his socks and shoes on, and he goes outside to exercise. He likes to run. Sam runs for a long time. After his run, he is hungry again.

True/False

Is the statement below true or false? Write T for true or F for false.

1. Sam is not hungry when he wakes up. _____
2. Sam eats eggs for breakfast. _____
3. Sam throws the banana peel on the floor. _____

4. Sam drinks milk because he is thirsty. _____

5. Sam goes outside to exercise after eating bananas. _____

Multiple Choice

Circle the correct answer

1. What does Sam eat for breakfast?

  a) Eggs

  b) Yogurt

  c) Banana

  d) Orange juice

2. What does Sam do after he eats the banana?

  a) Throws the peel in the garbage

  b) Leaves the peel on the counter

  c) Throws the peel on the floor

  d) Puts the peel back in the fridge

3. What does Sam drink for his thirst?

  a) Milk

  b) Orange juice

  c) Water

  d) Soda

4. What does Sam do after he drinks water?

  a) Goes to sleep

b) Goes outside to exercise

c) Watches TV

d) Takes a shower

5. What exercise does Sam enjoy?

a) Swimming

b) Biking

c) Running

d) Yoga

Fill in the blank

Fill in the blank with the sentences below.

1. Sam wants to _____ some food. eat / cook / bake

2. First Sam _____ the fridge. closes / cleans / opens

3. Sam sees bananas _____ his counter. in / at / on

4. Now Sam _____ thirsty. does / is / can

5. Sam likes _____ run. to / for / with

Answers

True/False 1. F 2. F 3. F 4. F 5. T

Multiple Choice 1. c) Banana 2. a) Throws the peel in the garbage 3. c) Water 4. b) Goes outside to exercise 5. c) Running

Fill in the blank 1. eat 2. opens 3. on 4. is 5. to

Story 6 **Jill Lost her Keys**

Jill always drives her car to work. She needs her keys, but she can't find them. She looks in her car. No keys. She looks on the table. No keys. She looks under the chair. No keys.

She asks her husband, "Where are my keys?"

"I don't know. I will help you look," he says. He looks on his desk. No keys. He looks in the bathroom. No keys.

Jill is mad. She wants her keys. She is late for work.

"I can drive you to work," her husband says.

They go to his truck. When they get in the truck, Jill sees her keys. "What!? Here are my keys!" she says.

"How did that happen?" her husband asks.

They don't know. Now Jill is happy. She takes the keys, and she gets out of the truck. She gets into her car. She starts her car. Then she drives to work. She is ten minutes late for work.

True/False

Is the statement below true or false? Write T for true or F for false.

1. Jill finds her keys in her car. _____
2. Jill's husband finds the keys in the bathroom. _____
3. Jill's husband suggests taking her to work. _____

4. Jill is early for work. _____

5. Jill's husband drives her to work. _____

Multiple Choice

Circle the correct answer

1. Where does Jill first look for her keys?

   a) In the car

   b) On the table

   c) Under the chair

   d) All of the above

2. What does Jill's husband suggest when they can't find the keys?

   a) Ordering a new set of keys

   b) Driving her to work

   c) Calling a locksmith

   d) Ignoring the problem

3. Where do they find the keys eventually?

   a) In the car

   b) On the table

   c) In the truck

   d) In the bathroom

4. How does Jill feel when she finds the keys?

a) Sad

b) Angry

c) Confused

d) Happy

5. How late is Jill for work?

a) Five minutes

b) Ten minutes

c) Fifteen minutes

d) Twenty minutes

Fill in the blank

Fill in the blank with the sentences below.

1. Jill drives _____ car to work. his / our / her

2. Jill looks _____ her car. under / in / on

3. Her husband looks on his _____. desk / bed / couch

4. Jill and her husband get _____ the truck. on / to / in

5. Jill is 10 minutes _____ for work. late / early / on time

_____

Answers

True/False 1. F 2. F 3. T 4. F 5. F

Multiple Choice 1. d) All of the above 2. b) Driving her to work 3. c) In the truck 4. d) Happy 5. b) Ten minutes

Fill in the blank 1. her 2. in 3. desk 4. in 5. late

Story 7 **Kairo's Bunny**

Kairo is five years old. He loves bunnies. He plays with his toy bunnies every day. Kairo wants a real bunny. He wants to feed it carrots and lettuce. Every day Kairo asks his mom for a real bunny. His mom always says no. One day she says yes. Kairo is so excited. He goes with his mom to the pet store. There are white bunnies. There are brown bunnies. There are gray bunnies. There are big bunnies. There are small bunnies. There are so many bunnies at the pet store. Kairo wants a brown bunny, and he wants a little bunny. Kairo chooses a brown, little bunny. It is so cute. His mom buys the bunny. She buys the bunny some bunny food. Kairo's dad makes a little bunny house. He paints it blue. Kairo plays with his bunny every day. He is so happy. He names his bunny Flopsy. Flopsy is his new best friend.

True/False

Is the statement below true or false? Write T for true or F for false.

1. Kairo is ten years old. _____
2. Kairo's mom always says yes when he asks for a real bunny. _____
3. Kairo chooses a white bunny at the pet store. _____
4. Kairo's dad makes a little bunny house for Flopsy. _____

5. Kairo names his bunny Fluffy. _____

Multiple Choice

Circle the correct answer

1. How old is Kairo?

a) Three years old

b) Five years old

c) Ten years old

d) Fifteen years old

2. What does Kairo want to feed his bunny?

a) Carrots and lettuce

b) Apples and bananas

c) Fish and meat

d) Chocolate and candy

3. What color bunny does Kairo choose?

a) White

b) Brown

c) Gray

d) Black

4. Who makes a little bunny house for Flopsy?

a) Kairo

b) Kairo's mom

c) Kairo's dad

d) Flopsy

5. What does Kairo name his bunny?

a) Fluffy

b) Hopper

c) Flopsy

d) Fuzzy

Fill in the blank

Fill in the blank with the sentences below.

1. Kairo is five years _____. young / birthday / old

2. Kairo wants a _____ bunny. real / fake / stuffed

3. There _____ white bunnies. is / are / am

4. Kairo's _____ makes a bunny house. dad / mom / brother

5. Kairo _____ with his bunny every day. eats / plays / swims

Answers

True/False 1. F 2. F 3. F 4. T 5. F

Multiple Choice 1. b) Five years old 2. a) Carrots and lettuce 3. b) Brown

4. c) Kairo's dad 5. c) Flopsy

Fill in the blank 1. old 2. real 3. are 4. dad 5. plays

Story 8 **Time to Clean**

Kim's house is so dirty. She needs to clean it. Kim has three kids. They are at school. Kim is home alone. She picks up her kids' toys. The kids' clothes are dirty, so Kim washes the clothes. The bathrooms are dirty, so she cleans the bathrooms. She wipes down the toilets. She wipes down the sinks. She cleans the mirrors. The kitchen is dirty, so she cleans the kitchen. She cleans the oven. She wipes off the refrigerator. She cleans the microwave. She washes the dishes. Her garbage is full, so Kim takes the garbage outside. The floors are dirty, so Kim vacuums the floors. Then she mops the floors. Finally her house is all clean. Kim is tired. Cleaning is a lot of work. She is so happy that her house is clean. Kim makes some tea. She sits in her living room and reads her book. She drinks her tea. Soon her kids will be home, and the house will be dirty again.

True/False

Is the statement below true or false? Write T for true or F for false.

1. Kim's kids help her clean the house. _____
2. Kim cleans the bathrooms before washing the dishes. _____
3. Kim mops the floors before vacuuming them. _____

4. Kim takes the garbage outside before cleaning the kitchen.
_____

5. Kim feels tired after cleaning the house. _____

Multiple Choice

Circle the correct answer

1. What does Kim do first when cleaning her house?

a) Washes the dishes

b) Vacuums the floors

c) Picks up her kids' toys

d) Cleans the bathrooms

2. What does Kim do after cleaning the bathrooms?

a) Washes the dishes

b) Vacuums the floors

c) Cleans the kitchen

d) Takes the garbage outside

3. What does Kim do after cleaning the kitchen?

a) Washes the dishes

b) Vacuums the floors

c) Mops the floors

d) Takes the garbage outside

4. What does Kim do after cleaning her house?

a) Sits in her living room

b) Reads a book

c) Drinks tea

d) All of the above

5. How does Kim feel after cleaning her house?

a) Angry

b) Frustrated

c) Tired

d) Excited

Fill in the blank

Fill in the blank with the sentences below.

1. Kim's house is so _____. dirty / old / new

2. Kim _____ home alone. am / are / is

3. Kim wipes _____ the toilets. to / down / up

4. Kim _____ tired. am / is / are

5. Kim _____ her tea. drinks / dumps / hates

Answers

True/False 1. F 2. T 3. F 4. F 5. T

Multiple Choice 1. c) Pick up her kids' toys 2. c) Cleans the kitchen 3. b) Vacuum the floors 4. d) All of the above 5. c) Tired

Fill in the blank 1. dirty 2. is 3. down 4. is 5. drinks

Story 9 **University**

John goes to university. It is his second year at university. He is a sophomore. He is studying to become a nurse. John goes to class on Monday, Tuesday, Wednesday, and Thursday. Friday is his day off. John studies on Friday. He studies biology, chemistry, math, and psychology. He has a lot of homework. University is hard. John lives in a dorm room, and he has one roommate. His roommate's name is Seth. Seth wants to be a teacher. John and Seth are best friends. Sometimes they study together. They like to study in the library. On Saturday John and Seth play video games in their dorm room. They order pizza every Saturday for dinner. Seth likes cheese pizza. John likes pepperoni pizza. John has a girlfriend. Her name is Katie. They met at university. On Sunday John and Katie go to church together. After church, they have a picnic in the park. John is a busy student. He does many things.

True/False

Is the statement below true or false? Write T for true or F for false.

1. John is studying to become a doctor. _____
2. John's day off from classes is Friday. _____

3. Seth wants to be a nurse like John. _____

4. John and Seth study together in the library. _____

5. John and Katie met at university. _____

Multiple Choice

Circle the correct answer

1. What is John studying to become?

　a) Doctor

　b) Teacher

　c) Nurse

　d) Engineer

2. How many days a week does John go to class?

　a) Three

　b) Four

　c) Five

　d) Six

3. What do John and Seth do on Saturdays?

　a) Play video games

　b) Go to the library

　c) Study biology

　d) Order kebabs

4. What kind of pizza does Seth like?

a) Cheese

b) Pepperoni

c) Hawaiian

d) Veggie

5. What do John and Katie do on Sundays?

a) Play video games

b) Go to church

c) Order pizza

d) Study together

Fill in the blank

Fill in the blank with the sentences below.

1. John is a _____. sophomore / junior / senior

2. John studies _____ Friday. in / on / at

3. John's roommate's name _____ Seth. is / am / are

4. _____ Saturday John and Seth play video games _____ their dorm room. In/on/ At/in/ On/in

5. They have a picnic _____ the park. with / to / in

Answers

True/False 1. F 2. T 3. F 4. T 5. T

Multiple Choice 1. c) Nurse 2. b) Four 3. a) Play video games 4. a) Cheese
5. b) Go to church

Fill in the blank 1. sophomore 2. on 3. is 4. On/in 5. in

Story 10 **Exercise**

Eve likes to exercise. She likes to run. She likes to do yoga. She likes to lift weights. Eve is athletic. Jude is Eve's friend. Jude doesn't like to exercise, but he likes to play soccer. Eve invites Jude to exercise with her. Eve wants to run in the park. Jude doesn't want to go, but he says yes because he likes Eve. He wants to ask Eve on a date. He thinks if he says yes to going running with Eve, she will say yes to a date. Eve is very good at running. She is running fast. Jude is so tired. He is very sweaty. Eve runs and runs. She doesn't stop. Her cheeks are pink, and she is breathing hard. Jude asks Eve for a break, so they sit on a bench in the park. Then Jude asks Eve on a date. Eve says no. Eve gets up and starts to run again. She is running so fast. Jude cannot catch her. He is sad. He wants to go on a date with Eve.

True/False

Is the statement below true or false? Write T for true or F for false.

1. Eve enjoys running, doing yoga, and lifting weights. _____
2. Jude enjoys exercising and running with Eve. _____
3. Jude agrees to go running with Eve because he wants to ask her on a date. _____

4. Eve agrees to go on a date with Jude. _____

5. Eve is slower than Jude when they run together. _____

Multiple Choice

Circle the correct answer

1. What does Eve enjoy doing for exercise?

a) Playing soccer

b) Running, yoga, and lifting weights

c) Lifting weights only

d) Yoga only

2. Why does Jude agree to go running with Eve?

a) Because he loves running

b) Because he wants to exercise

c) Because he wants to ask her on a date

d) Because he wants to beat her in a race

3. What does Jude ask Eve when they take a break from running?

a) If she wants to play soccer

b) If she wants to lift weights

c) If she wants to go on a date

d) If she wants to continue running

4. How does Eve respond to Jude's question about a date?

   a) She says yes.

   b) She says no.

   c) She laughs.

   d) She ignores him.

5. How does Jude feel when Eve starts running again?

   a) Sad

   b) Happy

   c) Excited

   d) Relieved

Fill in the blank

Fill in the blank with the sentences below.

1. Eve likes to _____ yoga. play/do/make

2. Jude doesn't like to exercise, _____ he likes to play soccer.

but / or / and

3. Jude wants to _____ Eve on a date. go / leave / ask

4. Jude _____ very sweaty. am / is / are

5. Jude _____ catch Eve. will / must / cannot

Answers

True/False 1. T 2. F 3. T 4. F 5. F

Multiple Choice 1. b) Running, yoga, and lifting weights 2. c) Because he wants to ask her on a date 3. c) If she wants to go on a date 4. b) She says no 5. a) Sad

Fill in the blank 1. do 2. but 3. ask 4. is 5. cannot

Story 11 **First Flight**

Jasmine is so excited. Today she is flying to California from Florida. She is going to California to see her sister. Her sister lives in California. Jasmine has never flown before. Today is her first flight. She packs her suitcase. It's summer, so she packs shorts, t-shirts, dresses, and sandals. She also packs two swimsuits and one jacket. She has a big purse. She puts her book in her purse.

Jasmine gets to the airport two hours before her flight. She checks in at the front desk. She gives the person at the desk her suitcase. She goes through security. Now she has to find her gate. It's gate A3. She finds her gate, and she sits down. She waits to board the airplane. Finally someone announces her flight. She waits in line. Then she hands the gate agent her boarding pass.

She gets on the plane and finds her seat. She has a window seat. She puts her purse under the seat in front of her. She is so nervous. No one sits next to her. She tries to read her book while she waits for the plane to take off.

Finally the plane takes off. Jasmine can't believe it. She is flying. She looks out the window. The cars look small. The houses look small, too. Jasmine sees the blue sky and the white clouds. She finally breathes normally. She closes her eyes and falls asleep. She wakes up when the captain says to prepare for landing. She sees the plane getting closer to the ground. The houses look bigger now. The plane lands, and Jasmine is so happy. When she gets off the plane, she sees her sister waiting for her. She runs to her sister and hugs her.

True/False

Is the statement below true or false? Write T for true or F for false.

1. Jasmine is flying to California to visit her friend. _____
2. Jasmine has flown before. _____
3. Jasmine packs winter clothes for her trip to California. _____
4. Jasmine's seat on the plane is an aisle seat. _____
5. Jasmine falls asleep before the plane takes off. _____

Multiple Choice

Circle the correct answer

1. What is Jasmine's reason for flying to California?

  a) To visit her sister

  b) To go on vacation

  c) To attend a business meeting

  d) To visit a friend

2. What does Jasmine pack in her suitcase?

a) Winter clothes

b) Swimsuits, shorts, t-shirts, and dresses

c) Coats and boots

d) Hats and gloves

3. Where does Jasmine wait to board the airplane?

a) In the bathroom

b) At the gate

c) In the security line

d) In the airport lounge

4. What type of seat does Jasmine have on the plane?

a) Middle seat

b) Aisle seat

c) Window seat

d) Front seat

5. What does Jasmine do when the plane lands?

a) Falls asleep

b) Reads a book

c) Prepares for landing

d) Sees her sister and hugs her

Fill in the blank

Fill in the blank with the sentences below.

1. Jasmine is flying _____ California. over / to / from

2. Her sister lives _____ California. in / on / at

3. Jasmine checks in _____ the front desk. on / from / at

4. Jasmine waits _____ line. in / on / at

5. Jasmine looks _____ the window. next to / out / to

Answers

True/False 1. F 2. F 3. F 4. F 5. F

Multiple Choice 1. a) To visit her sister 2. b) Swimsuits, shorts, t-shirts, and dresses 3. b) At the gate 4. c) Window seat 5. d) Sees her sister and hugs her

Fill in the blank 1. to 2. in 3. at 4. in 5. out

Story 12 **Victoria**

Victoria goes to her favorite coffee shop every Monday. She always orders a coffee with milk. In the winter, she drinks her coffee hot. In the summer, she drinks it with ice. She sits at a small table next to the window. She works on her laptop. She is a writer. She writes romance novels, and people love her books. Victoria is a best selling author. She knows everyone who works at the coffee shop, and they all know her. She doesn't need to tell them her order anymore. She sits down and they bring her a coffee with milk. Victoria writes for two hours, and then she stands up to stretch her legs. She goes outside, and she walks for ten minutes. After her walk, she goes back to the cafe. She writes for one more hour. Then she leaves.

She meets her friend at a restaurant for lunch. Victoria orders a chicken salad. She talks to her friend. Then she goes home. She feeds her dog, and she does her laundry. Then she watches TV and waits for her husband to come home. When he gets home, they eat dinner together. Victoria is tired, so she goes to sleep early.

True/False

Is the statement below true or false? Write T for true or F for false.

1. Victoria goes to her favorite coffee shop every Friday. _____

2. In the winter, Victoria drinks her coffee without ice. _____

3. Victoria works as a barista at the coffee shop. _____

4. Victoria is a best selling author of romance novels. _____

5. Victoria meets her friend at a coffee shop for lunch. _____

Multiple Choice

Circle the correct answer

1. What does Victoria order at her favorite coffee shop?

a) Hot chocolate

b) Tea

c) Coffee with milk

d) Iced tea

2. What does Victoria do after writing for two hours at the coffee shop?

a) Goes home

b) Takes a nap

c) Goes for a walk

d) Orders another coffee

3. What does Victoria do after meeting her friend at the restaurant?

   a) Goes home

   b) Goes shopping

   c) Goes to the movies

   d) Goes to the gym

4. What does Victoria do after going home?

   a) Feeds her cat

   b) Feeds her dog

   c) Feeds her fish

   d) Feeds her bird

5. What does Victoria do while waiting for her husband?

   a) Watches TV

   b) Goes for a walk

   c) Cleans the house

   d) Reads a book

Fill in the blank

Fill in the blank with the sentences below.

1. _____ the winter, she drinks her coffee hot. In / On / At

2. She works on her _____. phone / laptop / tablet

3. Victoria is a _____ selling author. best / worst / okay

4. Victoria writes _____ two hours. at / for / above

5. She meets her friend at a _____. restaurant / store / library

Answers

True/False 1. F 2. T 3. F 4. T 5. F

Multiple Choice 1. c) Coffee with milk 2. c) Goes for a walk 3. a) Goes home. 4. b) Feeds her dog 5. a) Watches TV

Fill in the blank 1. In 2. laptop 3. best 4. for 5. restaurant

Story 13 **A Simple Breakfast** TRUE STORY

I love breakfast. It's the most important meal of the day. Some days I eat oatmeal, and other days I eat eggs. I want to make oatmeal today, so I take a small pot and put it on the stove. I turn on the stove. Then, I put some oats and water in the pot. I add a little salt. I put a little maple syrup and a little coconut milk in the pot. The oats have to cook for five minutes. I use a wooden spoon to stir them. I stir them often, so they don't stick. After five minutes, I turn off the stove and put the oats in a bowl. I add blueberries, a banana, and almond butter to the bowl. I take a spoon from the drawer. Then I go to my table and sit down on the chair. I eat my oatmeal. When I am finished, I feel full. I put my dishes in the dishwasher. I wipe off the counter. Today is going to be a great day.

True/False

Is the statement below true or false? Write T for true or F for false.

1. Camille always eats eggs for breakfast. _____
2. Camille adds salt, maple syrup, and coconut milk to her oatmeal. _____

3. Camille cooks the oats for five minutes. _____

4. Camille eats her breakfast at the kitchen counter. _____

5. Camille feels hungry after eating her oatmeal. _____

Multiple Choice

Circle the correct answer

1. What does Camille make for breakfast in the story?

a) Pancakes

b) Omelet

c) Oatmeal

d) Cereal

2. How long does Camille cook the oats?

a) Three minutes

b) Five minutes

c) Ten minutes

d) Fifteen minutes

3. What does Camille add to her oatmeal?

a) Strawberries, honey, and milk

b) Blueberries, banana, and almond butter

c) Apples, cinnamon, and yogurt

d) Raisins, brown sugar, and cream

4. Where does Camille eat her oatmeal?

   a) In the living room

   b) In the bedroom

   c) At the kitchen table

   d) Outside in the garden

5. What does Camille do after eating her oatmeal?

   a) Goes for a run

   b) Washes the dishes

   c) Takes a nap

   d) Watches TV

Fill in the blank

Fill in the blank with the sentences below.

1. Breakfast is the most important _____ of the day.

dinner / meal / dessert

2. I put a pot _____ the stove. on / at / in

3. I put the oats _____ a bowl. on / at / in

4. I sit _____ on the chair. down / around / behind

5. I wipe _____ the counter. up / off / for

Answers

True/False 1. F 2. T 3. T 4. F 5. F

Multiple Choice 1. c) Oatmeal 2. b) Five minutes 3. b) Blueberries, banana, and almond butter 4. c) At the kitchen table 5. b) Washes the dishes

Fill in the blank 1. meal 2. on 3. in 4. down 5. off

Story 14 **My Hobbies** TRUE STORY

I have many hobbies. I like to learn new things. One of my hobbies is learning languages. I am studying Turkish now. It's a hard language. I watch videos in Turkish. I read easy books in Turkish. I talk to my friends on the phone in Turkish. Every day I study a little bit of Turkish.

I also love to exercise. Every morning I do something active. I walk or run, do yoga, or do a workout video on YouTube. I feel better when I move my body. I also enjoy the outdoors. My family likes to go to the beach or park together. Sometimes we go on hikes. It's very nice.

Traveling is another thing I really enjoy. My family likes to visit new countries together. We like to try new foods, meet new people, and practice speaking the language of the country we are in.

Another hobby of mine is reading. I love to read books. Every day I try to read one chapter or two from a book. Sometimes I read in other languages. Most of the time I read books in English.

I also love to bake. I like to bake muffins and cookies. I'm trying to learn how to bake sourdough bread. Sometimes my kids bake with me. I have a lot of hobbies.

True/False

Is the statement below true or false? Write T for true or F for false.

1. Camille's main hobby is painting. _____
2. Camille enjoys exercising outdoors with her family. _____
3. Camille reads books only in English. _____
4. Camille's family enjoys traveling to familiar places. _____
5. Camille bakes alone without involving her kids. _____

Multiple Choice

Circle the correct answer

1. What is one of Camille's hobbies?

a) Painting

b) Learning languages

c) Playing video games

d) Gardening

2. How often does Camille read books?

a) Every week

b) Every day

c) Every month

d) Every year

3. What activity does Camille enjoy doing with her family outdoors?

   a) Watching movies

   b) Going to the beach

   c) Playing board games

   d) Skiing

4. What is Camille trying to learn how to bake?

   a) Sourdough bread

   b) Cupcakes

   c) Brownies

   d) Pizza

5. What language is Camille currently studying?

   a) French

   b) Persian

   c) Turkish

   d) German

Fill in the blank

Fill in the blank with the sentences below.

1. I _____ studying Turkish now. am / is / are

2. I talk to my friends _____ the phone. through / in / on

3. My family likes to go _____ the beach. to / on / at

4. I love to _____ books. see / read / listen

5. I have a lot of _____. hobby / hobs / hobbies

Answers

True/False 1. F 2. T 3. F 4. F 5. F

Multiple Choice 1. b) Learning languages 2. b) Every day 3. b) Going to the beach 4. a) Sourdough bread 5. c) Turkish

Fill in the blank 1. am 2. on 3. to 4. read 5. hobbies

Story 15 **Sammy's Nighttime Routine**

Sammy is one year old. Sammy's mom's name is Valerie. She gives Sammy a bath every night before bed. He loves the bath. Valerie fills up the bathtub with warm water. She puts Sammy in the tub. Sammy splashes in the water, and he plays with his toys. He has a rubber duckie and some cups. He likes to fill the cups with water. Then he dumps the water out of the cups. Valerie uses shampoo to wash Sammy's hair. She uses a washcloth and soap to clean his body. Sammy plays in the bathtub for twenty minutes. Then Valerie takes him out, and he cries. He wants to play more. She wraps a big towel around him and sings him a song. Sammy stops crying. He likes songs. He smiles and wiggles his arms and legs. His mom puts his jammies on him. She gives him a bottle of milk. Sammy is a happy baby. Valerie reads Sammy a book and puts him in his crib. Sammy hugs his favorite animal. It's a stuffed bear. Sammy closes his eyes and goes to sleep.

True/False

Is the statement below true or false? Write T for true or F for false.

1. Sammy is two years old. _____

2. Valerie gives Sammy a bath every morning. _____

3. Sammy plays with a rubber duckie and cups in the bath. _____

4. Valerie uses soap but not shampoo to wash Sammy's body. _____

5. Sammy cries when Valerie sings him a song. _____

Multiple Choice

Circle the correct answer

1. What does Sammy play with in the bath?

a) Cars

b) Rubber duckie and cups

c) Blocks

d) Stuffed animals

2. How long does Sammy play in the bathtub?

a) Ten minutes

b) Twenty minutes

c) Thirty minutes

d) One hour

3. What does Valerie do to stop Sammy from crying after the bath?

a) Gives him a bottle of milk

b) Sings him a song

c) Gives him a toy

d) Ignores him

4. What does Valerie do after reading Sammy a book?

a) Takes him for a walk

b) Puts him in the bathtub

c) Puts him in his crib

d) Feeds him dinner

5. What does Sammy hug before he goes to sleep?

a) Stuffed bear

b) Stuffed cat

c) Washcloth

d) Soap bottle

Fill in the blank

Fill in the blank with the sentences below.

1. Valerie puts Sammy _____ the tub. in / on / at

2. Sammy fills the cups with _____. rocks / sand / water

3. Valerie takes Sammy _____ of the tub. under / out / from

4. Sammy _____ a happy baby. is / am / are

5. Valerie puts Sammy _____ the crib. in / on / at

_____

Answers

True/False 1. F 2. F 3. T 4. F 5. F

Multiple Choice 1. b) Rubber duckie and cups 2. b) Twenty minutes 3. b) Sings him a song 4. c) Puts him in his crib 5. a) Stuffed bear

Fill in the blank 1. in 2. water 3. out 4. is 5. in

Story 16 **My City** TRUE STORY

My city is named Viana do Castelo. It's not a very big city. 85,000 people live here. My city is twenty minutes from the border of Spain by car. It's an hour from Porto, which is a big city here in Portugal. Viana do Castelo is by the sea. There is also a big river in my city. I can see the river and the sea from my house. There is a bridge that goes across the river. My city has a historical center with many cute shops and restaurants. You can find many types of food in my city. There is Italian food, Indian food, Thai food, Japanese food, Portuguese food, and Brazilian food. There is one big shopping mall. There are many grocery stores. There is a train station and a bus station. My city has a lot of nature. There are mountains and hiking trails. Many people bike and walk in my city. There is a big hospital in my city. There are also many pharmacies. There are a lot of parks. My children love to play in the parks. There are some museums, and there is a beautiful church on a hill. There are some factories in my city, and there are many schools here. There is a community center and several hotels. There is a lot of wind here. My city is known for kitesurfing. Many tourists come here to kitesurf and surf.

True/False

Is the statement below true or false? Write T for true or F for false.

1. Viana do Castelo is a very large city. _____
2. The city is located an hour away from Porto. _____
3. There are many grocery stores and a big shopping mall in the city. _____
4. Viana do Castelo is located near the sea. _____
5. The city is not known for kitesurfing. _____

Multiple Choice

Circle the correct answer

1. How far is Viana do Castelo from the border of Spain by car?

   a) Ten minutes

   b) Thirty minutes

   c) Twenty minutes

   d) One hour

2. Which city is an hour away from Viana do Castelo?

   a) Porto

   b) Lisbon

   c) Madrid

   d) Barcelona

3. What is the city known for?

a) Skiing

b) Kitesurfing

c) Rock climbing

d) Snowboarding

4. What can be seen from Camille's house?

a) Mountains only

b) River only

c) Sea only

d) River and sea

5. What type of food can be found in Viana do Castelo?

a) Chinese food only

b) Indian food only

c) Portuguese, Italian, Thai, Japanese, and Brazilian food

d) Mexican food only

Fill in the blank

Fill in the blank with the sentences below.

1. There is a big river _____ my city. on / in / at

2. There _____ many grocery stores. am / is / are

3. Many people _____ in my city. bike / leave / move

4. My _____ is named Viana do Castelo. county / city / state

5. There are _____ lot of parks. a / some / many

Answers

True/False 1. F 2. T 3. T 4. T 5. F

Multiple Choice 1. c) Twenty minutes 2. a) Porto 3. b) Kitesurfing
4. d) River and sea 5. c) Portuguese, Italian, Thai, Japanese, and Brazilian
food

Fill in the blank 1. in 2. are 3. bike 4. city 5. a

Story 17 **Homeschooling** TRUE STORY

Because my family travels often, I choose to homeschool my children. Homeschooling means to educate your children from your home. Normally my children learn every morning Monday through Friday. My son Maddox is ten years old. He studies with an online program. Every day he reads and writes. He studies Portuguese and history. He also studies math and science. His favorite subject is science. My daughter Ivory is seven years old. Her main focus is reading and writing. She also loves art. She studies Portuguese like Maddox. My other son Kairo is five years old. This year he learned his ABC's. He learns with applications on his tablet. In the United States, children must attend school by the age of six. However, teaching your kids from home is legal and common. We often watch documentaries as a family. When we travel, we visit historical sites, museums, and other places that teach us about where we are visiting. We spend time reading books together, baking, and working on art projects. My kids also love the outdoors. We play at the park or the beach, and we go on nature walks. I think being outside is so important. Fresh air is good for us.

I like the freedom that homeschooling brings. I don't have to rush out the door in the morning. My children have a lot more time to play and just be kids. We can travel and have a lot more flexibility in our schedule. I don't know if I will homeschool forever, but for now it's the best choice for us.

True/False

Is the statement below true or false? Write T for true or F for false.

1. Homeschooling means educating children at home. _____
2. Maddox's favorite subject is history. _____
3. Ivory is learning math in homeschooling. _____
4. Camille doesn't value outdoor time for children. _____
5. Homeschooling is not legal in the United States. _____

Multiple Choice

Circle the correct answer

1. How old is Maddox?

  a) Seven

  b) Eight

  c) Nine

  d) Ten

2. What is Ivory's main focus in homeschooling?

  a) Math and science

  b) Reading and writing

c) Art and Portuguese

d) History and geography

3. How does Kairo learn his ABC's?

a) Through online programs

b) By reading books

c) With applications on his tablet

d) From watching TV

4. What is a common activity the family does when traveling?

a) Visits amusement parks

b) Watches movies

c) Visits historical sites and museums

d) Plays video games

5. What does Camille like about homeschooling?

a) Rushing out the door in the morning

b) More flexibility in her schedule

c) Limited outdoor time

d) Fixed curriculum

Fill in the blank

Fill in the blank with the sentences below.

1. My son Maddox _____ ten years old. am / is / are

2. His favorite _____ is math. subject / school / topic

3. Ivory is seven _____ old. weeks / years / months

4. Fresh air is good _____ us. for / on / at

5. Kairo is _____ years old. ten / seven / five

Answers

True/False 1. T 2. F 3. T 4. F 5. F

Multiple Choice 1. d) Ten 2. b) Reading and writing 3. c) With applications on his table 4. c) Visit historical sites and museums 5. b) More flexibility in her schedule

Fill in the blank 1. is 2. subject 3. years 4. for 5. five

Story 18 **Language Learning**

TRUE STORY

I really love to learn languages. I learned Spanish first, and I went to a formal school in Mexico. Then I learned Italian, Portuguese, and French on my own. I'm studying Turkish now. I learn languages because I love to learn about new cultures, and I love to meet new people. Learning new languages is a challenge for me, but I enjoy it. I use some applications like Duolingo and LingQ. I also watch a lot of YouTube videos. I write down many words, and I listen to videos, podcasts, and audiobooks. For me, the best way to learn is by being consistent and by finding things to study that I enjoy. When I have a basic understanding of the language, I start writing messages to natives. Then I leave voice messages. Finally I have language calls where I practice the language I'm learning, and I help my language partner learn English. Sometimes I pay for private lessons. Little by little, I learn more and more. It's an amazing feeling when I can talk to people in their native language. I think anyone can learn a language if they don't give up.

True/False

Is the statement below true or false? Write T for true or F for false.

1. Camille learned Spanish in a formal school in Spain. _____

2. Camille uses only one application, Duolingo, to learn languages. _____

3. Camille enjoys learning languages because it's easy for her. _____

4. Camille practices writing messages to native speakers as part of her language learning process. _____

5. Camille believes that anyone can learn a language if they give up easily. _____

Multiple Choice

Circle the correct answer

1. What is Camille currently studying?

   a) Spanish

   b) Italian

   c) Turkish

   d) French

2. How does Camille practice listening in the language she's learning?

   a) Watching TV shows

   b) Listening to podcasts and audiobooks

c) Reading newspapers

d) Writing letters to natives

3. What does Camille do when she has a basic understanding of a language?

a) Starts writing novels

b) Travels to the country

c) Writes messages to natives

d) Takes a break from learning

4. What does Camille sometimes pay for during her language learning journey?

a) Private lessons

b) Language apps

c) Books

d) Videos

5. What does Camille believe about learning a language?

a) It's impossible.

b) It's easy for everyone.

c) It requires consistency and enjoyment.

d) It's unnecessary.

Fill in the blank

Fill in the blank with the sentences below.

1. I went _____ a formal school _____ Mexico. on/in - to/in - at/on

2. I listen _____ podcasts. for / in / to

3. Sometimes I pay _____ private lessons. to / for / from

4. I love _____ meet new people. for / at / to

5. I really love _____ learn languages. to / for / too

Answers

True/False 1. F 2. F 3. F 4. T 5. F

Multiple Choice 1. c) Turkish 2. b) Listening to podcasts and audiobooks 3. c) Writes messages to natives 4. a) Private lessons 5. c) It requires consistency and enjoyment

Fill in the blank 1. to/in 2. to 3. for 4. to 5. to

Story 19 **The Appointment**

Lucia is so nervous. She lives in Maine. Spanish is her native language. She is learning English. She needs to make a doctor's appointment. She picks up her cell phone and dials the number for the doctor's office. She hears ringing.

"Hello. Crestview Medical. How can I help you?" a voice asks.

Lucia freezes. She can't remember anything.

"Hello. Hello," the voice continues.

"Uh, yes, hello," Lucia finally says. "Appointment, me, need."

"Okay, have you been here before? What is your name?" the woman asks.

"No. First time. Lucia Garcia," Lucia says.

"What is your date of birth and your reason for the visit?"

"Three August 1995. Stomach hurt," Lucia says.

"Okay, a doctor can see you today at 3:00. But come early to fill out some paperwork. Please bring your insurance card," the woman says.

"Please repeat. No understand," Lucia says.

"Today, come at 3:00. Bring your insurance card," the lady says slowly.

"Okay, okay, 3:00 I come. Thank you," Lucia sighs. She hangs up the phone. She takes a big breath. She had her first phone call in English. It was hard, but she did it.

*Note: I purposely wrote Lucia's responses with some mistakes.

1 - I need an appointment.

2 - No, it's my first time.

3 - August 3rd, 1995 (We always say the month followed by the day and then the year.)

4 - My stomach hurts.

5 - I don't understand.

6 - I will come / I will be there. (more native)

True/False

Is the statement below true or false? Write T for true or F for false.

1. Lucia's native language is English. _____

2. Lucia needs to make a dentist appointment. _____

3. Lucia successfully makes a doctor's appointment in English. ___

4. The woman on the phone repeats the appointment time in Spanish for Lucia. _____

5. Lucia feels relieved after her phone call in English. _____

Multiple Choice

Circle the correct answer

1. Where does Lucia live?

a) California

b) Maine

c) Texas

d) New York

2. What language is Lucia learning?

a) French

b) English

c) Spanish

d) Italian

3. What does Lucia need to bring to the doctor's appointment?

a) Passport

b) Insurance card

c) Credit card

d) Library card

4. What time is Lucia's appointment?

a) 12:00

b) 1:00

c) 2:00

d) 3:00

5. How does Lucia feel after making the appointment?

a) Anxious

b) Confused

c) Relieved

d) Frustrated

Fill in the blank

Fill in the blank with the sentences below.

1. She lives _____ Maine. at / on / in

2. She _____ learning English. will / is / want

3. What _____ your name? are / be / is

4. She hangs _____ the phone. at / on / up

5. It was hard, _____ she did it. but / from / or

Answers

True/False 1. F 2. F 3. T 4. F 5. T

Multiple Choice 1. b) Maine 2. b) English 3. b) Insurance card 4. d) 3:00
5. c) Relieved

Fill in the blank 1. in 2. is 3. is 4. up 5. but

Story 20 **Soccer Practice**

Dylan is 15 years old. He is a natural athlete. Every day after school, he has soccer practice. His team is very good. They have an amazing coach. Dylan is a goalkeeper. He works very hard. His coach thinks Dylan will get a scholarship to play soccer in college. Dylan's best friend is Ryan. Ryan is also a good soccer player. Ryan is the captain of the team. Practice is two hours long. They do push ups, situps, and squats. They sprint. They play against each other. They practice many kicking drills. Dylan drinks so much water during and after practice. After every practice, he drinks coconut water with lime and salt. His mom says it energizes him. His mom is very supportive of him playing soccer. She comes to every game. Dylan's dad can only come to some of his games because he works a lot. Dylan's team is halfway through the soccer season. They are going to play in the championship because they are very good.

True/False

Is the statement below true or false? Write T for true or F for false.

1. Dylan's team has a bad coach. _____
2. Dylan's mom comes to every game. _____

3. Dylan drinks coconut water with lime after practice. _____

4. Dylan's team will play in the championship. _____

5. Ryan is Dylan's brother. _____

Multiple Choice

Circle the correct answer

1. How old is Dylan?

 a) 10

 b) 15

 c) 20

 d) 25

2. What position does Dylan play in soccer?

 a) Forward

 b) Midfielder

 c) Goalkeeper

 d) Defender

3. Who is Dylan's best friend?

 a) Jack

 b) Ryan

 c) Ethan

 d) Lucas

4. What does Dylan's mom say energizes him after practice?

   a) Orange juice

   b) Coconut water with lime and salt

   c) Energy drinks

   d) Milkshake

5. Why can't Dylan's dad come to all of his games?

   a) He doesn't like soccer.

   b) He lives far away.

   c) He works a lot.

   d) He's busy playing soccer himself.

Fill in the blank

Fill in the blank with the sentences below.

1. He _____ soccer practice. is / has / have

2. His team _____ very good. are / is / wants

3. He drinks coconut water _____ lime and salt. in / at / with

4. She comes _____ every game. in / to / at

5. They are _____ to play in the championship. go / going / be

Answers

True/False 1. F 2. T 3. T 4. T 5. F

Multiple Choice 1. b) 15 2. c) Goalkeeper 3. b) Ryan 4. b) Coconut water with lime and salt 5. c) He works a lot

Fill in the blank 1. has 2. is 3. with 4. to 5. going

Story 21 **The Line**

Jed does not like waiting in lines. Today there is a big line at the grocery store. "Why is there only one lady working at the register?" he thinks. There are 10 people in line. All of them have their shopping carts filled with food. Someone cuts in line.

"Hey, no cutting. Go to the back of the line," a man says.

"But I only have two things to buy. I am in a hurry," the woman replies.

Finally they open another register. Half of the people move to the new line. Now there are five people in each line. Jed is third in line. There are two people in front of him. There are two people behind him. Finally it is Jed's turn. He puts his groceries on the belt. The lady at the register scans his groceries and places them in his cart. His total is $95. Jed pays with a credit card. Then he puts the food in his grocery bags and pushes his cart to his car. He puts his bags in the trunk. He drives to Starbucks because wants coffee. There is a big line. "Oh no," Jed thinks.

True/False

Is the statement below true or false? Write T for true or F for false.

1. Jed enjoys waiting in lines. _____
2. There were ten people in line at the grocery store. _____
3. The woman who cut in line had a full shopping cart. _____
4. Jed paid for his groceries with cash. _____
5. Jed drives to Starbucks because he wants a coffee. _____

Multiple Choice

Circle the correct answer

1. How many people moved to the new register when it opened?

   a) All ten

   b) Half of them

   c) None of them

   d) Only Jed

2. What does Jed do after paying for his groceries?

   a) Goes to the movies

   b) Drives to Starbucks

   c) Goes back home

   d) Returns his groceries

3. How much did Jed's groceries cost?

  a) $95

  b) $90

  c) $100

  d) $85

4. How does Jed pay for his groceries?

  a) Cash

  b) Credit card

  c) Check

  d) Debit card

5. Why does the woman cut in line?

  a) She is buying more groceries.

  b) She has to catch a bus.

  c) She is going to a meeting.

  d) She is in a hurry.

Fill in the blank

Fill in the blank with the sentences below.

1. There _____ 10 people in line. be / are / is

2. Someone cuts _____ line. on / at / in

3. Jed is third _____ line. in / on / at

4. He puts his groceries _____ the belt. on / in / from

5. He pushes his cart _____ his car. in / to / at

Answers

True/False 1. F 2. T 3. F 4. F 5. T

Multiple Choice 1. b) Half of them 2. b) Drives to Starbucks 3. a) $95 4. b) Credit card 5. d) She is in a hurry

Fill in the blank 1. are 2. in 3. in 4. on 5. to

FREE **AUDIOBOOK** DOWNLOAD HERE!

Step 1: Scan QR code - **Step 2:** Fill out form **Step 3:** Access Audio on Google Drive

SCAN FOR FREE AUDIO

https://bit.ly/freebeginnerenglish

Issues? Email me: audio@learnenglishwithcamille.com

FREE **FLASHCARD** DOWNLOAD HERE!

https://bit.ly/beginner-english-flashcards-pdf

(opens PDF FILE 7MB)

Story 22 **Sacramento**

Chloe is visiting Sacramento with her mom and dad. Chloe is seven years old. Chloe is wearing her favorite shorts and a red t-shirt with a heart on it. It's her first time in Sacramento. It's a day for adventure. It's summer and very warm. Chloe sees tall trees and big rivers. She goes to a magical castle called the California State Capitol. It has a golden roof that shines in the sun. They ride a train through the city. Chloe has so much fun. Next Chloe and her parents visit the Sacramento Zoo. Chloe loves the silly monkeys and big elephants. They walk a lot. Then they start to get hungry. Chloe eats pizza with her parents. Pizza is her favorite food. After they eat, they walk along the Tower Bridge. It's so pretty. It has sparkly lights on it. They stop for some ice cream. Her parents let her choose two flavors. Chloe chooses vanilla and strawberry. Chloe is so happy. Today is her favorite day.

True/False

Is the statement below true or false? Write T for true or F for false.

1. Chloe is visiting Sacramento with her grandparents. _____
2. Chloe is wearing a blue t-shirt with a star on it. _____

3. The California State Capitol has a silver roof. _____

4. Chloe's favorite food is pizza. _____

5. Chloe chooses chocolate and mint ice cream flavors. _____

Multiple Choice

Circle the correct answer

1. How old is Chloe?

a) Five years old

b) Seven years old

c) Ten years old

d) Twelve years old

2. What is the weather like in Sacramento?

a) Cold and snowy

b) Warm and sunny

c) Rainy and windy

d) Foggy and misty

3. What is Chloe's favorite food?

a) Pizza

b) Salad

c) Sandwich

d) Soup

4. What does the California State Capitol have on its roof?

a) Silver

b) Golden

c) Bronze

d) Copper

5. What flavors of ice cream does Chloe choose?

a) Chocolate and vanilla

b) Strawberry and chocolate

c) Vanilla and strawberry

d) Mint and chocolate chip

Fill in the blank

Fill in the blank with the sentences below.

1. It's her first time _____ Sacramento. in / to / at

2. She goes _____ a magical castle. at / to / in

3. Chloe loves _____ silly monkeys. a / the / this

4. Pizza _____ her favorite food. are / be / is

5. Chloe _____ so happy. is / are / be

Answers

True/False 1. F 2. F 3. F 4. T 5. F

Multiple Choice 1. b) Seven years old 2. b) Warm and sunny 3. a) Pizza
4. b) Golden 5. c) Vanilla and strawberry

Fill in the blank 1. in 2. to 3. the 4. is 5. is

Story 23 **Making Plans**

Bryce and Layla are a couple. They both work very hard. Bryce is an accountant, and Layla is an architect. They finally have a day off work tomorrow, so they are making plans to do something together. Layla is tired, so she wants to sleep in late. She also wants to clean the house and go to a yoga class. She wants to have a slow day. Bryce wants to wake up early to go for a hike. He wants to do some yard work. They both want to see a movie and eat dinner at a restaurant. They agree to each do what they want in the morning. They will meet at a restaurant for dinner. After dinner, they will go to the movie theater. Layla likes Thai and Indian food. Bryce likes Italian and Mexican food. Layla likes romance movies. Bryce likes action movies. They are so different. They can't decide where they will go. Finally they make a decision: Bryce will choose the restaurant, and Layla will choose the movie. They both win.

True/False

Is the statement below true or false? Write T for true or F for false.

1. Bryce and Layla are both doctors. _____
2. Layla wants to sleep in late on her day off. _____

3. Bryce wants to go for a hike in the morning. _____

4. Layla likes action movies. _____

5. They agree to each choose what they want to do in the morning. _____

Multiple Choice

Circle the correct answer

1. What does Layla want to do on her day off?

a) Go for a hike

b) Clean the house and go to a yoga class

c) Sleep in late

d) Work

2. What does Bryce want to do in the morning?

a) Clean the house

b) Go for a hike

c) Sleep in late

d) Watch a movie

3. How do they decide on their plans for the evening?

a) Layla chooses the restaurant and the movie.

b) Bryce chooses the restaurant, and Layla chooses the movie.

c) They flip a coin.

d) They argue about it.

4. What type of food does Layla like?

   a) Italian and Mexican

   b) Thai and Indian

   c) Chinese and Japanese

   d) American and French

5. What type of movie does Bryce like?

   a) Romance

   b) Action

   c) Comedy

   d) Horror

Fill in the blank

Fill in the blank with the sentences below.

1. Bryce and Layla _____ a couple. is / are / be

2. Bryce _____ an accountant. are / be / is

3. They both want _____ see a movie. to / go / too

4. Layla _____ tired. is / are / be

5. She wants _____ clean the house. too / to / two

Answers

True/False 1. F 2. T 3. T 4. F 5. T

Multiple Choice 1. b) Clean the house and go to a yoga class 2. b) Go for a hike 3. b) Bryce chooses the restaurant, and Layla chooses the movie 4. b) Thai and Indian 5. b) Action

Fill in the blank 1. are 2. is 3. to 4. is 5. to

Story 24 **George**

Aria is a foreigner. She is from Guatemala, but she lives in Texas. The food, the people, the language, and the sizes of things are so different for her. Texas has very big trucks and very big people. Aria's native language is Spanish. She is still learning English. She is a nanny for a family that has three kids. She lives with the family. She has her own bedroom and bathroom.

Every day she cooks, cleans, and watches the toddler, whose name is George. George is very silly. He likes to play with toy cars. He doesn't like to wear clothes. He always has only a diaper on. George has one sister. Her name is Molly. George has one brother. His name is Trent. Trent and Molly go to school every day, and George stays at home with Aria. George and Aria play outside a lot. George picks flowers, and he gives them to Aria. George likes to pet his dog Scruffy. George laughs a lot. Everything is fun for him. Aria and George have a special bond. Aria thinks George is a very special little boy.

True/False

Is the statement below true or false? Write T for true or F for false.

1. Aria is from Texas. _____

2. Aria is fluent in Spanish. _____

3. George likes to wear clothes. _____

4. Aria watches three kids. _____

5. George's dog's name is Fluffy. _____

Multiple Choice

Circle the correct answer

1. What is Aria's native language?

   a) English

   b) Spanish

   c) French

   d) German

2. How many kids does the family have?

   a) One

   b) Two

   c) Three

   d) Four

3. What does George like to play with?

a) Dolls

b) Toy cars

c) Blocks

d) Puzzles

4. Where do Trent and Molly go every day?

a) School

b) Park

c) Library

d) Grocery store

5. What does George like to do outside?

a) Read books

b) Pick flowers

c) Play video games

d) Watch TV

Fill in the blank

Fill in the blank with the sentences below.

1. She lives _____ Texas. at / in / from

2. Aria's native language _____ Spanish. be / is / are

3. She lives _____ the family. in / at / with

4. George _____ very silly. be / are / is

5. George _____ one brother. have / has / is

Answers

True/False 1. F 2. T 3. F 4. T 5. F

Multiple Choice 1. b) Spanish 2. c) Three 3. b) Toy cars 4. a) School 5. b) Pick flowers

Fill in the blank 1. in 2. is 3. with 4. is 5. has

Story 25 **Passport Control**

It's Barbara's first time traveling to the United States. She is visiting her aunt in Virginia. Barbara is traveling alone from Brazil. She has her passport and her visa with her. She gets off the plane and walks to passport control. The officer asks her some questions. He asks her how long she is going to stay in the United States, her address, and why she is visiting. Barbara tells him that she is visiting her aunt and staying for one month. She gives the officer the correct address. Her English is very good because she has been practicing a lot. The officer stamps her passport and tells her to have a nice time. Barbara takes a deep breath. She made it through. She is so excited to see her aunt and to experience new things in Virginia. She wants to practice her English every day, make new friends, and try new foods. Most of all, she is thankful for a vacation.

True/False

Is the statement below true or false? Write T for true or F for false.

1. Barbara is traveling with her cousin from Brazil. _____
2. Barbara's aunt lives in Virginia. _____
3. Barbara's English skills are poor. _____

4. Barbara doesn't have her visa with her. _____

5. Barbara plans to stay in the United States for six months. _____

Multiple Choice

Circle the correct answer

1. Where is Barbara visiting her aunt?

   a) California

   b) Virginia

   c) Texas

   d) New York

2. How long does Barbara plan to stay in the United States?

   a) One week

   b) One month

   c) Six months

   d) One year

3. What does the officer ask Barbara at passport control?

   a) Her favorite color

   b) Her age

   c) Her address and length of stay

   d) Her shoe size

4. Why is Barbara visiting the United States?

   a) To study

   b) To work

   c) To see her aunt

   d) To go sightseeing

5. What does Barbara want to do during her visit?

   a) Avoid speaking English

   b) Try new foods and make friends

   c) Stay indoors all day

   d) Never leave her aunt's house

Fill in the blank

Fill in the blank with the sentences below.

1. She is visiting her aunt _____ Virginia. at / on / in

2. Her English _____ very good. does / is / are

3. Barbara _____ excited to see her aunt. are / does / is

4. She wants _____ practice her English every day. to / and / too

5. She _____ thankful for a vacation. are / be / is

Answers

True/False 1. F 2. T 3. F 4. F 5. F

Multiple Choice 1. b) Virginia 2. b) One month 3. c) Her address and length of stay 4. c) To see her aunt 5. b) Try new foods and make friends

Fill in the blank 1. in 2. is 3. is 4. to 5. is

Story 26 **Hotel Reservation**

Jess and Camille are sisters. They are driving from Washington to Michigan to visit their parents in Michigan. It's a very long trip. Jess is driving, and she is so tired. Camille is sleeping in the car. It's raining outside. Finally Jess says that she cannot drive anymore. Camille wakes up and says that she will look for a hotel online. She sees one ten minutes away. They pull up to the hotel and park the car. They go to the front desk and ask the receptionist if there is a room available. The receptionist looks at her computer and says yes. She tells them there is a room with one king bed or a room with two queen beds. Jess and Camille choose the room with two queen beds. The receptionist tells them that there is a swimming pool and a gym that they can use. She says that breakfast is complimentary; they don't have to pay any extra money for breakfast. Then she asks them for one of their driver's licenses. Jess shows her driver's license to the receptionist. Then the receptionist asks how they would like to pay. Camille pays with her credit card. The receptionist has them sign some papers, and then she gives them their room key. "Have a great stay," she says.

True/False

Is the statement below true or false? Write T for true or F for false.

1. Jess and Camille are friends traveling together. _____

2. They are driving from Michigan to Washington. _____

3. Jess is too tired to continue driving. _____

4. They choose a room with one king bed. _____

5. Breakfast is not included in their stay. _____

Multiple Choice

Circle the correct answer

1. Who is driving the car?

   a) Camille

   b) Their parents

   c) Jess

   d) A friend

2. What does Camille do when Jess says she can't drive anymore?

   a) She takes over driving.

   b) She looks for a hotel online.

   c) She falls asleep.

   d) She calls their parents.

3. How many beds are in the room they choose?

   a) One king bed

b) Two queen beds

c) One queen bed

d) Three twin beds

4. How does Camille pay for the room?

a) Cash

b) Check

c) Credit card

d) Debit card

5. What services does the hotel offer?

a) Swimming pool and gym

b) Breakfast and dinner

c) Spa and sauna

d) Tennis court and golf course

Fill in the blank

Fill in the blank with the sentences below.

1. Jess and Camille _____ sisters. is / are / be

2. They _____ driving from Washington to Michigan. is / are / do

3. The receptionist looks _____ her computer. to / in / at

4. Breakfast _____ complimentary. does / are / is

5. She gives them _____ room key. there / their / they're

Answers

True/False 1. F 2. F 3. T 4. F 5. F

Multiple Choice 1. c) Jess 2. b) She looks for a hotel online. 3. b) Two queen beds

4. c) Credit card 5. a) Swimming pool and gym

Fill in the blank 1. are 2. are 3. at 4. is 5. their

Story 27 **At the Library**

Sheldon loves to go to the library. He goes there every day after school. Reading is his favorite hobby. Sheldon loves to read about many things. He reads both fiction and nonfiction books. He reads about animals and science. He also likes to learn about different cultures. The librarian Mrs. Sawyer knows his name. "What can I help you with today, Sheldon?" she asks.

"I don't know. It's strange, but today I don't know what I want to read," he tells her.

"Sometimes that happens. We have some new books on the shelves. Go have a look. I will be here if you need help," she says, smiling warmly.

Sheldon looks for a book to read. Finally he finds a book that looks interesting. It's called *Around the World in Eighty Days*. He sits in his favorite chair and starts to read.

"Sheldon, Sheldon," a voice calls. He looks up to see Mrs. Sawyer. "I see you are reading a good book. The library is closing now. Would you like to check that book out?"

"Yes, I would," says Sheldon. He has to know if Fogg will finish his adventure around the world or not. Sheldon checks out the book and runs home.

True/False

Is the statement below true or false? Write T for true or F for false.

1. Sheldon goes to the library every day after school. _____

2. Mrs. Sawyer is the librarian. _____

3. Sheldon only reads fiction books. _____

4. Sheldon finds a book titled *Around the World in Eighty Days.* _____

5. Sheldon checks the book out before leaving the library. _____

Multiple Choice

Circle the correct answer

1. What is Sheldon's favorite hobby?

   a) Playing video games

   b) Watching movies

   c) Reading

   d) Playing sports

2. Who helps Sheldon find a book to read?

   a) His friend

   b) His teacher

   c) His librarian, Mrs. Sawyer

   d) His parents

3. What book does Sheldon find interesting?

a) *Around the World in Eighty Days*

b) *Harry Potter and the Sorcerer's Stone*

c) *The Hunger Games*

d) *Diary of a Wimpy Kid*

4. What does Mrs. Sawyer ask Sheldon before the library closes?

a) If he needs help finding a book

b) If he wants to buy a book

c) If he wants to check out the book

d) If he needs a ride home

5. Why does Sheldon check out the book?

a) He wants to know if Fogg will finish his adventure.

b) He wants to return it later.

c) He wants to keep it forever.

d) He wants to show it to his friend.

Fill in the blank

Fill in the blank with the sentences below.

1. Sheldon loves to go _____ the library. at / to / on

2. Reading _____ his favorite hobby. am / is / are

3. Sheldon looks _____ a book to read. for / to / from

4. He _____ in his favorite chair. stands / lies / sits

5. The library _____ closing now. will / are / is

Answers

True/False 1. T 2. T 3. F 4. T 5. T

Multiple Choice 1. c) Reading 2. c) His librarian, Mrs. Sawyer 3. a) *Around the World in Eighty Days* 4. c) If he wants to check out the book 5. a) He wants to know if Fogg will finish his adventure.

Fill in the blank 1. to 2. is 3. for 4. sits 5. is

Story 28 **Online Dating**

Ella is thirty years old. She is single. She is using a dating app because she wants to meet someone new. She receives many new messages, but she isn't attracted to the men who send her messages. One day Romeo messages her. Ella opens her eyes wide. He is so cute. He has dark brown hair and green eyes. Ella messages him back. They write messages back and forth. Ella learns that Romeo is Italian. Romeo is a pilot. He is thirty-four years old. He lives in Boston, not too far from Ella. Romeo and Ella start having phone conversations. Ella loves Romeo's cute accent. One month later, they have a videochat. They have a very strong connection. Ella starts to learn Italian. They decide to meet in person. Romeo is taller in real life. Ella wonders how he is still single. She believes in fate. She really, really likes Romeo. She thinks about him all the time. The good news is that he feels the same. They fall in love.

True/False

Is the statement below true or false? Write T for true or F for false.

1. Ella is using a dating app because she is married. _____
2. Romeo is from Italy. _____

3. Romeo is a chef. _____

4. Ella and Romeo have phone calls. _____

5. They decide to never meet in person. _____

Multiple Choice

Circle the correct answer

1. What is Romeo's profession?

  a) Chef

  b) Pilot

  c) Doctor

  d) Teacher

2. Where does Romeo live?

  a) New York

  b) Boston

  c) Los Angeles

  d) Chicago

3. How do Ella and Romeo communicate before meeting in person?

  a) Through letters

  b) Through phone calls and video chats

  c) Through carrier pigeons

  d) Through telepathy

4. What language does Ella start to learn?

  a) French

  b) Italian

  c) Spanish

  d) German

5. How do Ella and Romeo feel about each other?

  a) They don't care about each other.

  b) They hate each other.

  c) They love each other.

  d) They don't like each other.

Fill in the blank

Fill in the blank with the sentences below.

1. She _____ single. is / does / are

2. She isn't attracted _____ the men. from / to / about

3. He _____ dark brown hair. have / has / is

4. Romeo _____ a pilot. be / is / are

5. She believes _____ fate. about / on / in

Answers

True/False 1. F 2. T 3. F 4. T 5. F

Multiple Choice 1. b) Pilot 2. b) Boston 3. b) Through phone calls and video chat

4. b) Italian 5. c) They love each other.

Fill in the blank 1. is 2. to 3. has 4. is 5. in

Story 29 **Christmas Dinner**

Lacey loves Christmas dinner. Every year her whole family celebrates together. Including children, there are seventeen people in her family. Lacey is hosting Christmas at her house. Lacey's family always has good food for Christmas dinner. This year her parents are making a big turkey. Her brother Jeremy is bringing ham and sweet potatoes. Her sister Kate is making mashed potatoes and green beans. Her other sister Jill is baking bread and pies.

Lacey decorates the table with special place settings. She lights white candles in the center. She writes little name cards by each plate. She sets out nice wine glasses. She sets two bottles of red wine on the table. She puts on Christmas music in the background. Her husband lights a fire in the fireplace. Her children are playing with their new toys by the Christmas tree. She smiles as the doorbell rings. She is so excited for dinner. She is also excited for her family gift exchange. Every year they buy one special present for someone in the family. She loves the pink scarf she bought for her sister Kate. It starts to snow outside. It's going to be a beautiful evening.

True/False

Is the statement below true or false? Write T for true or F for false.

1. Lacey's family doesn't celebrate Christmas dinner together. ____
2. Lacey's family consists only of adults. _____
3. Lacey's brother Jeremy is making mashed potatoes and green beans. _____
4. Lacey's husband lights a fire in the fireplace. _____
5. Lacey's family does not exchange gifts during Christmas. _____

Multiple Choice

Circle the correct answer

1. How many people, including children, are in Lacey's family?
   a) Ten
   b) Twelve
   c) Fifteen
   d) Seventeen

2. Who is hosting Christmas?
   a) Lacey's parents
   b) Lacey's sister Kate
   c) Lacey herself
   d) Lacey's brother Jeremy

3. What is Lacey's sister Jill baking?

  a) Bread and pies

  b) Ham and sweet potatoes

  c) Mashed potatoes and green beans

  d) Turkey

4. What does Lacey's husband do?

  a) Decorates the table

  b) Cooks the turkey

  c) Lights a fire in the fireplace

  d) Sets out wine glasses

5. What does Lacey love about the Christmas gift exchange?

  a) She loves the snow outside.

  b) She loves the special presents.

  c) She loves playing with her children.

  d) She loves the Christmas music.

Fill in the blank

Fill in the blank with the sentences below.

1. There _____ seventeen people in her family. does / are / is

2. She _____ candles in the center. lights / starts / turns

3. She puts _____ Christmas music. in / on / at

4. She _____ so excited for dinner. are / is / be

5. It starts _____ snow outside. from / is / to

Answers

True/False 1. F 2. F 3. F 4. T 5. F

Multiple Choice 1. d) Seventeen 2. c) Lacey herself 3. a) Bread and pies
4. c) Lights a fire in the fireplace 5. b) She loves the special presents.

Fill in the blank 1. are 2. lights 3. on 4. is 5. to

Story 30 **Freckles**

Josh loves basketball. Every day he practices outside in his driveway. Today, he is playing with his friend Dan. Josh dribbles the ball, he shoots the ball, and then he passes the ball to his friend Dan.

One day Josh's parents buy him a cat. Josh loves the cat. He names the cat Freckles. There is only one problem. The cat always bites Josh's ankles. Josh wants to go outside, but Freckles is outside. Josh is afraid to go outside. He tells his mom he is scared, but she says, "Oh it's just a little cat. Don't be silly."

So Josh goes outside to play, and Freckles is waiting for him. Freckles bites Josh's ankles. This time, Freckles bites Josh so hard. Now Josh is bleeding. Josh starts to shout and cry. Josh's mom comes running to him. His mom feels terrible. "What a naughty little cat!" she says. She puts bandages on Josh's ankles. She brings the cat back to the shop. "Sorry Freckles, you have to go," she says.

Josh doesn't like cats anymore. His mom comes home with a new dog. Josh names it Ruby.

True/False

Is the statement below true or false? Write T for true or F for false.

1. Josh practices basketball indoors. _____
2. Josh's friend's name is Dan. _____
3. Josh's parents buy him a cat. _____
4. Freckles, the cat, bites Josh's ankles. _____
5. Josh's mom keeps Freckles even after Freckles bites Josh. _____

Multiple Choice

Circle the correct answer

1. Where does Josh practice basketball?

   a) At the park

   b) In his driveway

   c) Indoors

   d) At the gym

2. What does Josh name the cat his parents buy him?

   a) Spot

   b) Freckles

   c) Ruby

   d) Dan

3. What does Freckles do to Josh when Josh goes outside to play?

a) Bites his ankles

b) Plays with him

c) Ignores him

d) Meows loudly

4. How does Josh's mom react when Freckles bites Josh?

a) She laughs.

b) She scolds Josh.

c) She apologizes and puts bandages on his ankles.

d) She ignores Josh.

5. What pet does Josh's mom bring home after returning Freckles?

a) A cat

b) A dog

c) A rabbit

d) A fish

Fill in the blank

Fill in the blank with the sentences below.

1. He _____ playing with his friend. will / are / is

2. There _____ only one problem. is / are / be

3. Josh _____ afraid to go outside. are / am / is

4. Don't _____ silly. be / are / is

5. What _____ naughty little cat. a / the / one

Answers

True/False 1. F 2. T 3. T 4. T 5. F

Multiple Choice 1. b) In his driveway 2. b) Freckles 3. a) Bites his ankles
4. c) She apologizes and puts bandages on his ankles. 5. b) A dog

Fill in the blank 1. is 2. is 3. is 4. be 5. a

Congrats! What's next?

Be sure and listen to these stories again and again. Use the audio to train your ear and improve listening comprehension. Repetition is a great way for your brain to pick up patterns in speech and you will recognize more and more as you continue to read and listen.

Get ready for my Intermediate English stories!

My intermediate English Stories book is coming soon. If you want to know when it launches watch my Instagram or join my email list:

FREE ENGLISH RESOURCES

Can you help me out?

Review this book - If you bought this book on Amazon or my website, could you leave a review? Honest positive reviews really help others find it and benefit from it! Let's help the world learn English!

Find an error or have a suggestion? Message me at book@learnenglishwithcamille.com

Learn with Camille on Social

Instagram - @camillehanson

Tiktok - @LearnEnglishwithCamille

Youtube - @LearnEnglishwithCamille

Facebook - @LearnEnglishwithCamille

Hi, I'm Camille.

Thanks for reading my Beginner English Short Stories Book. I look forward to continuing to learn English together!

❤ Camille

More English Resources by Camille

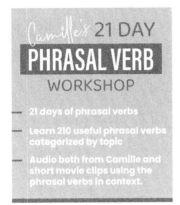

INVEST IN YOUR ENGLISH TODAY!

learnenglishwithcamille.com

Notes

Made in the USA
Las Vegas, NV
03 November 2024

11084848R00075